D1178904

JUST
BE
YOU.

summersdale

JUST BE YOU

Summersdale Publishers Ltd
46 West Street
Chichester
West Sussex
PO19 1RP
UK

www.summersdale.com

Printed and bound in Croatia

ISBN: 978-1-78685-233-5

Substantial discounts on bulk quantities of Summersdale books are available to corporations, professional associations and other organisations. For details contact general enquiries: telephone: +44 (0) 1243 771107 or email: enquiries@summersdale.com.

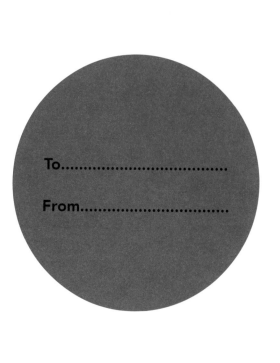

To.....................................

From.................................

Be yourself
for yourself.

Nothing can dim the light
which shines from within.

Maya Angelou

YOU DON'T HAVE TO BE PERFECT TO BE WONDERFUL.

Just when the caterpillar thought the world was ending, it became a butterfly.

English proverb

Be as kind to yourself
as you are to your friends.

Be in love with your life.
Every minute of it.

Jack Kerouac

You don't need to change,
just to love who you are.

Life isn't about finding yourself; it's about creating yourself.

Anonymous

INSTEAD OF TRYING TO MAKE SEVEN BILLION PEOPLE HAPPY, TRY MAKING ONE PERSON HAPPY: YOU.

Those who wish to sing
always find a song.

Swedish proverb

SPEAKING
KINDLY TO
PLANTS HELPS
THEM GROW:
IMAGINE WHAT
BEING KIND TO
YOURSELF DOES.

Be happy. It's one way of being wise.

Colette

You are enough.

THE MOST IMPORTANT KIND OF FREEDOM IS TO BE WHAT YOU REALLY ARE.

Jim Morrison

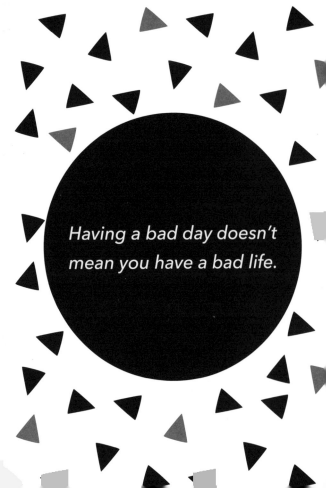

Having a bad day doesn't mean you have a bad life.

LIVE ALL YOU CAN; IT'S A MISTAKE NOT TO.

Henry James

PEOPLE DON'T REMEMBER WHAT YOU DO OR SAY,

THEY ONLY REMEMBER HOW YOU MAKE THEM FEEL.

You are at your most
powerful when you
don't seek approval.

If I am not for myself,
who is for me?

Hillel

The best person you can be is yourself.

You yourself, as much as anybody in the entire universe, deserve your love and affection.

Anonymous

What others think of
you is their choice;
what you think of
yourself is your choice.

THE FINAL FORMING OF A PERSON'S CHARACTER LIES IN THEIR OWN HANDS.

Anne Frank

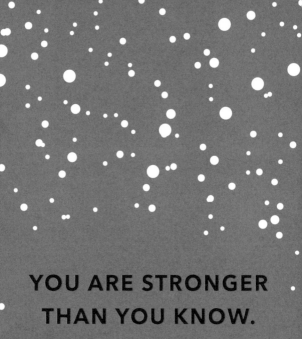

YOU ARE STRONGER
THAN YOU KNOW.

It takes courage to grow up and become who you really are.

E. E. Cummings

Everything you need –
your courage, strength,
compassion and love
– is already within you.

You have to be unique
and different and shine
in your own way.

Lady Gaga

PUT
YOURSELF
FIRST.

Your self-worth is defined by you. You don't have to depend on someone telling you who you are.

Beyoncé

*Confidence
is like a muscle.
The more you use it,
the stronger it gets.*

IF YOU CAN'T LAUGH, YOU WON'T MAKE IT.

Jennifer Love Hewitt

Self-love is the greatest medicine.

Happiness is not a goal;
it is a by-product.

Eleanor Roosevelt

WHEN THERE ARE SHADOWS, LOOK TO THE LIGHT.

It's not selfish to
love yourself, take care
of yourself and to make
your happiness a priority.
It's a necessity.

Mandy Hale

Build your happiness on your own foundations, not other people's.

Owning your story
is the bravest thing
you will ever do.

Brené Brown

Don't just be good
to others, be good
to yourself too.

If you obey all the rules,
you miss all the fun.

Katharine Hepburn

FORGET WHAT YOU AREN'T. LOVE WHAT YOU ARE.

How you love yourself
is how you teach
others to love you.

Rupi Kaur

YOU'RE
BRAVER
THAN YOU
BELIEVE.

Do not forget your
duty to love yourself.

Søren Kierkegaard

There is always a way.

ALWAYS LAUGH WHEN YOU CAN.

IT IS CHEAP MEDICINE.

Lord Byron

*Continue to
love yourself and
believe in yourself;
you are worth it.*

A TRUE FRIEND IS SOMEONE WHO LETS YOU HAVE TOTAL FREEDOM TO BE YOURSELF.

Jim Morrison

YOU'RE ONLY CONFINED BY THE WALLS YOU BUILD YOURSELF.

BREAK DOWN YOUR WALLS.

We should stop defining each other by what we are not, and start defining ourselves by who we are.

Emma Watson

You can be the ripest, juiciest peach in the world, and there's still going to be somebody who hates peaches.

Dita Von Teese

Being alive is a special occasion.

Do what you can,
with what you have,
where you are.

Theodore Roosevelt

YOU ARE THE HERO OF YOUR STORY.

The question isn't who is going to let me, it's who is going to stop me.

Ayn Rand

I LOVE THE PERSON
I WAS BORN TO BE.

You must be the change you wish to see in the world.

Mahatma Gandhi

Your life is a work of art –
it deserves to be seen.

Our aspirations are
our possibilities.

Samuel Johnson

FIND
THE JOY
IN LIVING.

Whoever is happy will
make others happy too.

Anne Frank

Make every minute count.

YOU GROW UP
THE DAY YOU
HAVE THE FIRST
REAL LAUGH
AT YOURSELF.

Ethel Barrymore

Do not tolerate
disrespect,
not even from
yourself.

Knowledge is
limited. Imagination
encircles the world.

Albert Einstein

Be who you've always
wanted to be.

IT IS NOT THE MOUNTAINS WE CONQUER, BUT OURSELVES.

Edmund Hillary

Turn your hopes

into realities.

A head full of dreams
has no space for fears.

Anonymous

Look for the flowers
that grow up through
the cracks.

It is not in the stars
to hold our destiny
but in ourselves.

William Shakespeare

YOU ARE A
WARRIOR,
NOT A
WORRIER.

Put your future in good hands – your own.

Anonymous

MAKE CONFIDENCE YOUR SUPERPOWER.

What you think of
yourself is much more
important than what other
people think of you.

Seneca

Uniqueness is what
makes you beautiful.

TO BE BEAUTIFUL
MEANS TO BE
YOURSELF.
YOU DON'T NEED
TO BE ACCEPTED
BY OTHERS.
YOU NEED TO
ACCEPT
YOURSELF.

Thích Nhất Hạnh

Inhale confidence.
Exhale self-doubt.

I SAY IF I'M
BEAUTIFUL.
I SAY IF I'M
STRONG.
YOU WILL NOT
DETERMINE MY
STORY - I WILL.

Amy Schumer

You've got this.

Talk to yourself
like you would to
someone you love.

Brené Brown

I AM A POWERHOUSE.

I AM
INDESTRUCTIBLE.

I'm a big believer in accepting yourself the way you are and not really worrying about it.

Jennifer Lawrence

**You can't build
joy on a feeling
of self-loathing.**

Don't be afraid to speak up for yourself. Keep fighting for your dreams!

Gabby Douglas

OUR FIRST AND LAST LOVE IS SELF-LOVE.

Attitude is everything.

Diane von Fürstenberg

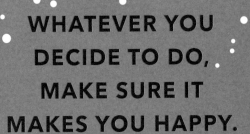

WHATEVER YOU DECIDE TO DO, MAKE SURE IT MAKES YOU HAPPY.

Mastering others
is strength.
Mastering yourself
is true power.

Lao Tzu

Don't give up.

We don't even know how strong we are until we are forced to bring that hidden strength forward.

Isabel Allende

THEY NEEDED A HERO, SO THAT IS WHAT THEY BECAME.

WHAT MATTERS MOST IS HOW WELL YOU WALK THROUGH THE FIRE.

Charles Bukowski

Dream big, work hard, stay focused and surround yourself with good people.

Ignore self-doubt
and inner conflict.
Dwell on positive
thoughts.

Lailah Gifty Akita

Be fearless in
the pursuit of
what sets your
soul on fire.

No one can make you
feel inferior without
your consent.

Eleanor Roosevelt

WHEN YOU LOVE WHAT YOU HAVE, YOU HAVE EVERYTHING YOU NEED.

You only live once,
but if you do it right,
once is enough.

Mae West

Now and then it's good to pause in the pursuit of happiness and just be happy.

You don't get harmony when everybody sings the same note.

Anonymous

Happiness will never come to those who fail to appreciate what they already have.

Every man is the architect of his own fortune.

Appius Claudius Caecus

YOU ARE A GOOD THING, JUST THE WAY YOU ARE.

Go confidently in
the direction of your
dreams. Live the life
you have imagined.

Henry David Thoreau

YOU ARE A
SONG, SO MAKE
SURE YOU
ARE HEARD.

Doubt is a killer. You just have to know who you are and what you stand for.

Jennifer Lopez

SOMEONE ELSE'S OPINION OF YOU

DOES NOT HAVE TO BECOME YOUR REALITY.

ALWAYS BE A FIRST-RATE VERSION OF YOURSELF, INSTEAD OF A SECOND-RATE VERSION OF SOMEBODY ELSE.

Judy Garland

I can overcome
any obstacle
life throws at me.

If you think you're too small to have an impact, try going to bed with a mosquito.

Anita Roddick

Everything is going
to be OK.

THE ONLY THING IMPORTANT IS RIGHT NOW. BEING HERE,

ALIVE AND PRESENT IN THIS MOMENT.

Never dull your shine
for somebody else.

Tyra Banks

Today is the first day of the rest of your life.

YOU'RE WORRIED ABOUT WHAT-IFS.
WELL, WHAT IF YOU STOPPED WORRYING?

Shannon Celebi

No beauty
shines brighter
than that of a
good heart.

The important thing is
not what they think of me,
but what I think of them.

Queen Victoria

WHATEVER IS GOOD FOR YOUR SOUL, DO THAT.

I think that sometimes being fearless is having fears but jumping anyway.

Taylor Swift

Every day is a fresh start.

I have come to believe
that caring for myself
is not self-indulgent.
Caring for myself is
an act of survival.

Audre Lorde

HAVING CONFIDENCE ISN'T ABOUT NOT BEING SCARED; IT'S ABOUT PUTTING YOURSELF OUT THERE ANYWAY.

THE MOST COURAGEOUS ACT IS STILL TO THINK FOR YOURSELF. ALOUD.

Coco Chanel

*Take it one
day at a time.*

It's OK to stop
doing and just be.

Lori Deschene

I am not
beautiful like you.
I am beautiful
like me.

I don't like to gamble,
but if there's one
thing I'm willing to
bet on, it's myself.

Beyoncé

IF YOU'RE
SEARCHING
FOR THAT ONE
PERSON THAT
WILL CHANGE
YOUR LIFE,
TAKE A LOOK IN
THE MIRROR.

The potential for greatness lives within each of us.

Wilma Rudolph

Be yourself.
There is no one better.

I am a slow walker,
but I never walk back.

Abraham Lincoln

Dear self, today
you will shine.

You are magnificent
beyond measure, perfect
in your imperfections,
and wonderfully made.

Abiola Abrams

WHAT IF YOU SIMPLY DEVOTED EVERY DAY TO LOVING YOURSELF MORE?

If we all did the things we are capable of doing, we would literally astound ourselves.

Thomas Edison

THINGS MAY
BE MESSY BUT
SOMETIMES
MAKING A MESS
IS A LOT OF FUN.

Turn your face towards
the sun and the shadows
will fall behind you.

Maori proverb

YOU ARE AMAZING. YOU ARE BRAVE. YOU ARE STRONG.

DON'T LET THEM

TAME YOU.

Isadora Duncan

If you don't start now, you will always be in the same place.

DON'T BELIEVE THE SKY IS THE LIMIT;

THERE ARE FOOTPRINTS ON THE MOON.

When you know yourself
you are empowered.
When you accept yourself
you are invincible.

Tina Lifford

Don't look back.
You're not going that way.

It is never too late to
be what you might
have been.

George Eliot

Just breathe.

Most folks are about
as happy as they make
up their minds to be.

Anonymous

PUSH
YOURSELF.

Just say yes,
just say there's nothing
holding you back.

Zoella

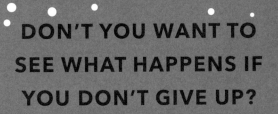

DON'T YOU WANT TO SEE WHAT HAPPENS IF YOU DON'T GIVE UP?

Stop wishing
and start doing.

THERE IS JUST ONE LIFE FOR EACH OF US: OUR OWN.

Euripides

If you're interested in finding out more about our books, find us on Facebook at **Summersdale Publishers** and follow us on Twitter at **@Summersdale**.

www.summersdale.com

Image credits

p.9, 40, 72, 105, 137 © yellowpixel/Shutterstock.com
p.18, 50, 82, 115, 147 © Alex Landa/Shutterstock.com
p.24, 56, 89, 121, 153, 160 © Alex Kednert/Shutterstock.com
p.28, 60, 93, 125, 157 © Oxy_gen/Shutterstock.com